The Art of Creating PARETO ANALYSIS

A Complete End-to-End Guide to Understand Pareto Charts and Easily Create them in Excel

RAHUL G. IYER

THE ART OF CREATING PARETO ANALYSIS

CONTENTS

CHAPTER 1: REAL LIFE ANECDOTE # 1

Pareto Analysis is one of the finest statistical tools. It will help you identify those defects that cause maximum impact. Allow me to share a real-life anecdote of the effectiveness of Pareto Analysis.

A disclaimer before we begin: Although this story belongs to the service industry, the practices shared here can easily be replicated in manufacturing or any other industry.

The Story Begins

I was working as a Six Sigma expert for a New York based bank. I operated from Pune, India but frequently visited the headquarters on account of business. On one of my visits to our headquarters in New York, the business unit head of our bank expressed a concern relating to one of his businesses. He mentioned that the quality score of one of their products has a target of 100% but they have not been meeting that target. His business process was consistently underperforming. The client was terribly upset because of this issue. He also mentioned that the business manager was recently summoned for this issue, but the manager has not been able to find the root-cause yet. I was in New York for another two days and he asked me to investigate the issue further and share my thoughts on the solution.

The Analysis

I requested the data that I could get for this process and that evening I sat doing the analysis. Now, in most scenarios, if you are improving the Quality Scores, you will look at the Quality Score metric. But I had a hunch that other process improvement experts must have already analyzed this metric. So, I preferred to analyze a rather crude metric and that was analyzing the number of defects. I looked at the number of defects by:

1) The name of each team member who processed the transactions.
2) By Team
3) By Shift
4) By Month
5) By Week and
6) By Day of the Week

I used Pareto Analysis to look at each of the above. Nothing really yielded for the first five options. But when I did the Pareto Chart of the number of defects by day of the week, Viola! I found this issue.

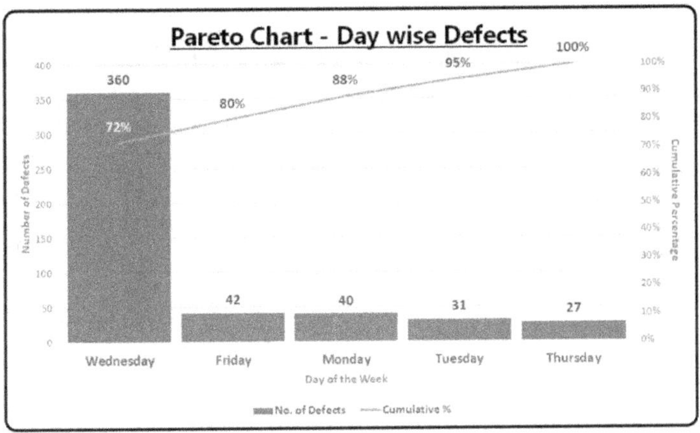

Interpreting the Chart and Identify the Root-Cause

This chart shows the number of defects in the business process are significantly high on Wednesdays compared to any day of the week. Wednesday's contribute to 72% of the total defects. And this was the same pattern for multiple weeks.

So, something was going wrong on Wednesday for sure. Since the business manager was already summoned by the Business Unit head, I did not want him to be involved in my investigation. I had a few colleagues who worked as mid-level managers in that business process, but if I approached them, they might raise an alarm. I was scheduled to fly back from New York to Pune on Friday night and it was Wednesday evening already, so I could not wait until next Wednesday to see what was happening on the shop floor.

It was critical for me to see what was really going on in the shop floor. So, I requested the Risk and Control team to share the CCTV footage of four random weeks – Monday through Friday. After seeking the approval from the Business Unit head, the CCTV footages arrived.

I started to review these footages for each day of the week. And as the Pareto Analysis had revealed that Wednesday is a problem, I did find the problem. So, this is what I found:

1) On Monday, Tuesday, Thursday, and Friday – the entire shop floor was quiet, calm and involved in work. There was no noise, no unnecessary loitering of employees, and the process discipline was well within control.

2) However, on Wednesdays, I could see a lot of commotion on the shop floor. Music was being played. Employees were moving around, chatting with each other, laughing out loud, etc. I am not saying that the employees were not working, they were. But the atmosphere was rather too relaxed compared to other days of the week.

Identification of Root-Cause goes to the next level:

Now, I was puzzled with another question – what really happened on Wednesday for the atmosphere to be more relaxed? That's where I found that the manager's office was always occupied by him on Monday, Tuesday, Thursday, and Friday, but it was unoccupied on Wednesday. So, that means the manager was not in office on Wednesday. I looked at the attendance report and found that the manager was marked present on Wednesdays.

So, what was really going on?

Upon speaking to other business managers in his circle, I found a few more things. The bank that I worked for was a big organization with its offices in more than 200 locations. Pittsburgh was one of the key locations. Every Wednesday, the corporate jet of our bank was open for employees to fly from New York to Pittsburgh for free. And on Thursday morning, the jet would be back from Pittsburgh to New York. Since Pittsburgh was a key location, this facility of using the Corporate

Jet was provided to employees to cut down costs to fly from New York to Pittsburgh during the week.

This manager took the Corporate Jet each Wednesday and visited his mom who lived in Pittsburgh. On that day, he worked from home. Then, on Thursday, the manager would be back to New York's office.

Now this arrangement was ok because every employer must respect employee's work life. But because of the manager's absence from the shop floor on Wednesdays, the following things happened:

1) The discipline on the shop floor was relaxed.
2) This led to more commotion on the floor.
3) The relaxed atmosphere caused the employees to be less vigilant while processing transactions.
4) As a result, they missed on meeting the target of 100% quality score.

My job was to perform the analysis and identify the root cause. I did that and shared the report including the CCTV footages to the business unit head. He was not too surprised that I got him the real root-cause, in fact he was confident about my ability to get to the root of the issue and that's why he had assigned me to this task. But he was too surprised at how unique the root-cause was? After that meeting, I took my flight from New York to Pune as scheduled.

Results

The next week, on my weekly call with the business unit head, he mentioned that the business manager was confronted with the issue. He was shown the reports and observations. And while he could continue meeting his mom in Pittsburgh on Wednesday's each week, his direct reports were made responsible to manage floor discipline.

In the next two weeks, the business unit head further shared that the business process was now meeting their target of 100% Quality Score after the corrective actions were implemented. So, our root-cause identification was right on target. In a nutshell, it was the Pareto Analysis that made the real difference to this solve this business problem.

As usual, I was commended for this effort. The business unit head wrote a compliment to my boss. My boss was happy. Our department was happy. I was happy too, because I could become the James Bond of my business process without using guns and expensive cars.

Well, with Pareto Analysis, you can solve many business problems like these. And you will learn how to create and use Pareto Analysis in your business process. Please note that the Pareto Analysis is a simple tool. Hence, please do not expect this book to be very long. My objective is to provide you with the details of What is Pareto Analysis? How to Create It? And also help you understand its real-life applications through these real-life anecdotes that are sprinkled throughout this course. I am sure you will love this book.

CHAPTER 2: INTRODUCTION

Hey there, thank you for buying this book — a warm welcome. It is a little weird to share my warm regards in the second chapter. I did that because I wanted to introduce you to the power of the Pareto Analysis through the real-life anecdote, right in the first chapter. You will see more of these real-life stories sprinkled in the later chapters too.

Let's talk about this chapter. Here, you will go through an overview of the entire book.

This book is divided into three key sections:

• What is Pareto Analysis?
• When to use Pareto Analysis?
• How to create Pareto Analysis?

You will begin your journey with the first section: What is Pareto Analysis? Here, you will go through:

• Book Introduction (which is this chapter)
• You will seek an answer to the question: What is Pareto Analysis?

The next section is: When to use Pareto Analysis? In this section, you will understand how Pareto Analysis looks like? You will learn about the 4W's that are tackled by a Pareto Analysis. You will also learn about the ideal data type of X and Y variables where Pareto Analysis can be applied and used.

The third and final section of this book is: How to Create a Pareto Analysis? In this section, you will learn "How to Create a Pareto Chart in Excel 2016?" You will be provided the data and you will be taken through the step-by-step instructions of creating your first Pareto Chart (using this data).

Additional Bonus

Your learning will not be complete until you know how to use Pareto Analysis in real-life environment. Hence, as described earlier, throughout this book, I have sprinkled my real-life anecdotes. I hope you will love them.

So, that is how the entire book is arranged. There are 3 sections and each of the section is divided into specific bite-sized chapters.

This book is unique because of its practical knowledge and easy to follow steps. After completing this book, you will master this tool and understand how to identify specific causes that have maximum impact on the business process.

If you have any questions that need to be addressed immediately, please email us at programs@aigproexcellence.com. My customer friendly team will be happy to respond to you as soon as possible.

This book is ideal for professionals who are working in manufacturing as well as the service industry. It is also suitable for beginners or freshers or those looking for a job in the market.

Kindly be advised that this book is NOT about an overview of the Pareto Analysis. This book teaches you all the details to analyze any data using the Pareto Analysis. You will get step-by-step instructions. It is about knowing this tool end-to-end. It is truly a masterclass and will help you master Pareto Analysis and use it in any business to understand the causes that affect your process and its performance.

CHAPTER 3: WHAT IS PARETO ANALYSIS?

You may have heard a saying that eighty percent of wealth lies with twenty percent of people. This saying is applicable to your work environment too. You can say:

80% of the Defects are due to 20% of the Causes

This is the 80-20 rule or the Pareto principle or the Pareto Analysis.

The 80-20 rule was coined by an economist. His name, Vilfredo Pareto, from Italy. He coined this term around the 1890s. You can imagine that this rule is being used even today after more than 110 years. That is the power of this principle.

CHAPTER 4: WHEN TO USE THE PARETO ANALYSIS?

Let's say you work in the phone banking division of a retail bank. Your bank has this phone banking department in five other locations. The bank account holders call the phone banking service to resolve their banking queries.

Due to high number of complaints, your bank is losing revenue. As a result, your bank launched a Lean Six Sigma project to reduce the number of complaints. The first question that will think is "What the most common complaint is?"

Here is the Pareto Chart of complaints. Let's discuss this chart in detail.

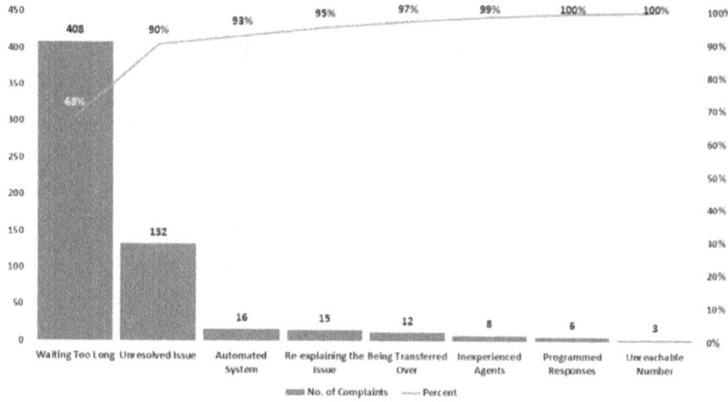

The chart has two axis – one on the left (the primary axis) and the other on the right (the secondary axis).

- The top line is the cumulative percentage line.
- This line references the axis to the right of the chart.
- The actual frequency count is on the left or the primary axis.
- This count is shown by the height of each bar for each category. These categories or bars are prioritized from highest to lowest.

In this chart, the "Waiting Too Long" is the biggest complaint category, with sixty-eight percent of the total number of complaints. The "Unresolved Issue" is the second highest at about twenty-two percent. Together, the "Waiting Too Long" and the "Unresolved Issue" make up ninety percent of the total number of complaints. The other categories make up about ten percent or less.

So, the project team must focus on analyzing the problem of "Waiting Too Long" first. Once that is analyzed, and if the time and resources permit, the team can look at analyzing the second problem: "Unresolved Issue."

Also, where or which locations account for the most number

of complaints. Here is the Pareto Chart of complaints by location.

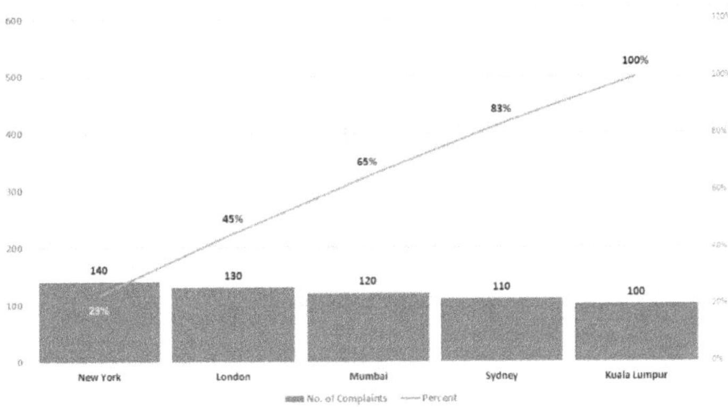

None of the locations stand out. There is no 80-20 effect. Does it mean this chart is of no use? No. What it does show is that the number of complaints is not specific to any one location. More importantly, it shows that complaints are a systemic problem across all locations of the bank's phone banking division.

By asking what type of complaint and whether the number of complaints is the highest for a particular location, you are stratifying the key metric data. In a nutshell, you are stratifying the data by asking "What" and "Where" in this example.

Now, in addition to stratifying the data by what and where you can also stratify using "Who" and "When." Such as using the Pareto Chart of complaints by team or by day of the week.

A pro tip on stratification – when using a Pareto Chart, you can ask the four W's:

• Who?

- What?
- Where?
- When?

Please see that we have not added the question "Why" in the four W's. This is because you will ask the Why question after answering the Who, What, Where, and When questions. You will ask this "Why" when further investing the root-cause.

In our example, the total count of complaints can be divided into categories such as by location, type, teams, and the day of the week.

A Pareto chart can be used for categorical count data.

So, we now conclude this chapter. Before you begin to learn How to Create a Pareto Chart, it is time to read another Real-Life Anecdote.

CHAPTER 5: REAL LIFE ANECDOTE # 2

Here I share another real-life story of how Pareto Analysis had a massive impact to solve a business problem. Let's begin:

A disclaimer before we begin: Although this story belongs to the service industry, the practices shared here can easily be replicated in manufacturing or any other industry.

The Story Begins

I was working as a Six Sigma professional for one of the largest Internet Service Providers based in the U.K. I operated from Pune, India and worked as an internal consultant to help solve business problems across all the locations of this business.

As you would probably know, Customer Satisfaction Scores is considered one of the key metrics for the Internet Service Providers. If the provider is not meeting the customer satisfaction levels, customers can easily switch to competitors resulting in loss of business as well as loss of reputation.

Since this was one of the biggest Internet Service company in the U.K., they had staffed about 2,500 employees in their customer service team. This team was responsible to meet the customer satisfaction score of at least 65%. Now, for the past 2 years, this team was able to meet the threshold of 65%, however, for the past 12 weeks i.e., 3 months, the team was consistently falling short of achieving this target. The internal quality team tried to analyze the data and identify all the possible root-causes, but they were not hitting the right root-cause. And that's where I received a phone call from the Head of the Business to look into the issue.

I did not have to travel to the U.K. office because we all work in a truly globalized world. I just had to make a few phone calls to request for the Customer Satisfaction Score data. In return, I received megabytes and megabytes of excel spreadsheets for 2,500 people for the past 6 months. The volume was huge. Finding the root-cause appeared to be like finding a needle in a haystack. That is where your experience and expertise come in.

I will share one guru mantra: Whenever you deal with complex or voluminous issues, try to use simple tools and techniques to find the trends in the available data. With this approach, there is a high chance that you will find some anomalies that will lead you to the right root-causes. Leave the complex statistical analysis for simple situations.

Situations like these where the Customer Satisfaction Scores were being met earlier and have dropped suddenly, you must know that there are two possibilities:

1) There is a shift that has occurred in the business and how the transactions are handled. Without this significant shift, the change in the satisfaction scores is not possible. All you must do is to identify what has caused the shift to occur.

2) The second thing to remember is that since the business process is huge (about 2,500+ people), you may want to start with the analysis of People related changes. I will elaborate on

this a little.

The Analysis

When analyzing people related changes, you can do multiple things. You can segment people:

1) By Teams
2) By the Shift they work in
3) By Sub-business Process or by the Type of Work handled by them
4) By Week or by day of the week
5) By Season
6) By their Tenure

So, I segmented the people data in all these categories and created Pareto charts. The top five categories did not yield any significant insights. But the last category – i.e., the tenure of people yielded the necessary insights.

The chart looked like this:

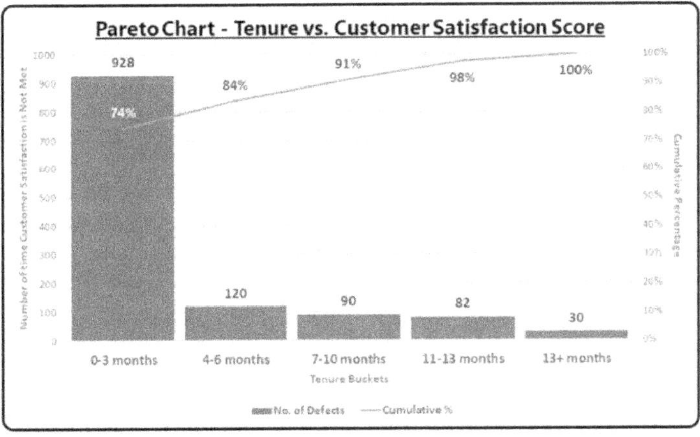

Interpreting the Chart and Identifying the Root-Cause

You will find that the tenure of 0-3 months (basically, the new hires) had the highest number of situations where customer satisfaction was not being met. Now, you may say, Rahul, it is obvious that new hires will take time to go through the learning curve and not meet the threshold. I completely agree. But the next key question is: How many new hires exist? And I found that the process had over 700 new hires. Whoa! That is almost 30% of the process population.

Identification of Root-Cause goes to the next level:

Now another key question pops up. Does this business process generally have so many new hires each quarter? I pulled up the hiring requisition report and found that there are generally 25 to 30 positions that are filled each quarter.

So, why was there a need of hiring 700 people? Upon further discussion with the HR, it was found that another big telecom player had emerged in U.K.'s telecom market. This player had started poaching employees of this organization giving them higher pay, more perks, good positions, among others. Hundreds of aspiring employees left this organization and joined the new one creating a need to hire 700+ new employees.

So, that was the real story of what had happened. 30% of the process was filled with new hires and as they started processing transactions, the overall customer satisfaction scores dropped significantly below the threshold.

It is important to confirm if your root-cause identification is correct. All I had to do was remove the customer satisfaction score data for the new hires and recalculate the revised satisfaction scores. Viola! The process was well above 65% target when the new hire data was removed.

This is an interesting insight. Now, the next question that popped up in my mind was – the head of this department had mentioned that the internal process analysts analyzed the data. So why were they not able to find this root-cause? When I spoke to them, I found that they were not aware about the new hire scenario. But then I was not aware of the new hire situation either. But the right understanding and interpretation of data and asking the right "Why" questions led me to this root-cause.

Action Identification and Implementation

I reported my observations to the head of the business. Practically, you cannot expect the new hires to meet the required goals immediately. But the team came up with an ingenious solution.

They routed only a limited type of transactions to the new hires rather than routing all types of transactions to them. Many of these (limited) type of transactions were high volume cases. Because the new hires now started handling only a few types of cases, their learning curve was shortened, and they started meeting the required goal of 65% customer satisfaction scores.

I also took a crash course for the internal business analysts explaining them how to interpret data from given charts and graphs, ask the right "Why" questions and reach the root-causes.

This was extremely helpful and valuable to the business.

Results

The implemented actions improved the Customer Satisfaction Scores in the next two weeks. Woohoo! Because I was involved in a good project with the process experts, I formed a good working bond with all of them. The head of business dropped a complimentary note to my boss. My boss was happy. My department was happy. And I was happy too because my annual appraisal discussion was around the corner. I was indeed given a good rating and I loved the annual increment. A huge annual bonus was the cherry on the icing. Woohoo!

In a nutshell, a simple tool like Pareto Analysis helped this business process significantly. This is the power of this tool. When used right, this tool can work wonders and help businesses reach root-causes significantly faster than expected.

CHAPTER 6 CREATE A PARETO CHART IN EXCEL

Creating a Pareto Chart in Excel 2016 is easy. At the same time, it is tedious too. It involves many minor steps. Explaining them only through text and paragraphs will be crude and difficult to follow. Hence, I have chosen to share this knowledge using two techniques:

Technique # 1:

If you do not prefer to read a lot of text and would want to have step-by-step directions using a downloadable pdf and/or gain access to an exclusive video lecture, please use any of the below resources:

Resources # 1: Access PDF only

The below link will provide you FREE access to a downloadable pdf that provides step-by-step instructions (with images) to create a Pareto Chart:

https://pages.aigproexcellence.com/pareto/download-pdf-only

Resource # 2: Access the Video Lecture + PDF

The below link will provide you FREE access to a video lecture as well as the downloadable pdf. Both the resources will provide step-by-step instructions to create a Pareto Chart in Excel 2016:

https://pages.aigproexcellence.com/pareto/access-video-lecture-and-pdf

Technique # 2 is not continued further as you will get all the required details in any of the above-mentioned resources.

Technique # 2:

This technique does not require you to access any downloadable free content. All you must do is copy the data shown in the below diagram in your spreadsheet. While copying the data in the spreadsheet, please ensure the data in each row and column matches exactly with that of the one in the image.

	A	B	C	D	E	F	G	H	I	J
1	Complaint Reason	No. of Complaints	Cumulative	Percent			Complaint Reason	No. of Complaints	Cumulative	Percent
2	Waiting Too Long	408	408	68%			Automated System	16		
3	Unresolved Issue	132	540	90%			Being Transferred Over	12		
4	Automated System	16	556	93%			Inexperienced Agents	8		
5	Re-explaining the Issue	15	571	95%			Programmed Responses	6		
6	Being Transferred Over	12	583	97%			Re-explaining the Issue	15		
7	Inexperienced Agents	8	591	99%			Unreachable Number	3		
8	Programmed Responses	6	597	100%			Unresolved Issue	132		
9	Unreachable Number	3	600	100%			Waiting Too Long	408		
10		600								

Then follow all the steps outlined next.

Introduction to this data

The data provided in the table is the count of complaints of a telephone banking service. The complaint reasons column articulates the type of complaint, and the number of complaints column shows the count of those complaint types.

You will find two tables listed on this spreadsheet. The table on the left (let's call it Table 1) is from columns A to D. The table on the right (let's call it Table 2) is from columns G to J. Table 1 is a reference table. You will learn to transform Table 2 to make it look similar to Table 1 using the next steps.

Step # 1: Sort the Data

To sort the data, please follow these steps:

1) Click and select **cell H2**

2) Click **"Data"** in the menu bar

3) Click **"ZA"** in the Data ribbon

It is important to put column H in descending order to create the Pareto Chart.

Step # 2: Calculate the Cumulative Total

Step 2.1: *Calculation of Cumulative Total will be in Column I.*

Follow the below steps:

1) Click and select **cell H2**

2) Use formula **"=H2"**

3) Hit **Control + Enter**

You will get **408** as the total.

Step 2.2:

The continued step consists of adding the formula that is equal to previous cumulative plus the latest entry. Please see the image. To do this:

1) Click and select cell **I3**

2) Use formula **"=I2+H3"**

3) Hit **Control + Enter**

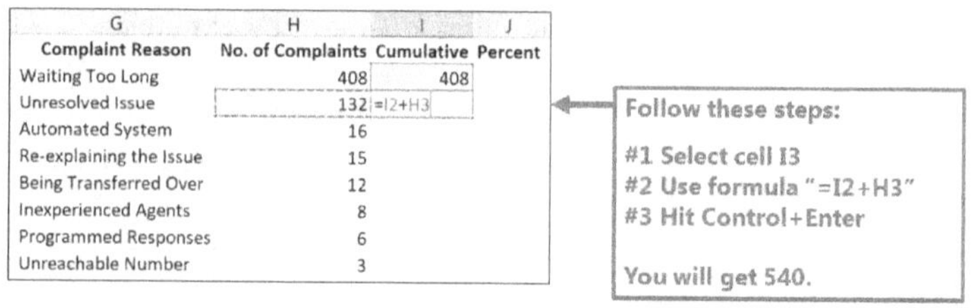

Step 2.3:

For all the remaining rows, you want to put in the same formula. Follow the below steps to do so:

1) Select cell **I3**

2) **Double-click the square dot** on the bottom right corner of cell I3

Column I will be filled with the cumulative values.

Step 2.4:

We also want the total of column H to reflect in cell H10. This is because we do want to know the total number of complaints for our next calculation.

To get the total in cell H10, use the below steps:

1) Click and select cell **H10**

2) Click the **Formulas Tab** in the menu bar

3) Click **Autosum** in the Formulas ribbon

4) Hit **Control + Enter**

You will get **600** as the total.

Step # 3: Calculate the Percent Column

Step 3.1:

You will calculate the percent based on the cumulative entry divided by the total. To do this, follow the below steps:

1) Select cell **J2**

2) Use formula **"=I2/H10"**

3) By keeping cursor on H10, hit **"F4"** (this will make the value absolute)

4) Hit **Control + Enter**

G	H	I	J
Complaint Reason	No. of Complaints	Cumulative	Percent
Waiting Too Long	408	408	=I2/H10
Unresolved Issue	132	540	
Automated System	16	556	
Re-explaining the Issue	15	571	
Being Transferred Over	12	583	
Inexperienced Agents	8	591	
Programmed Responses	6	597	
Unreachable Number	3	600	
	600		

Follow these steps:

#1 Select cell J2
#2 Use formula "=I2/H10
#3 By keeping cursor on H10, hit "F4"
#4 Hit Control+Enter

After hitting F4, the H10 will be changed to H10

Step 3.2:

You will calculate the percent based on the cumulative entry divided by the total. To do this, follow the below steps:

1) Click and select cell **"J2"**

2) **Double-click the square dot** on the bottom right corner of cell J2

Column J will be filled with percent values.

Step # 4: Create the Pareto Chart

Follow the outlined steps to create the Pareto Chart:

1**) Select the columns:** Complaint Reason, No. of Complaints, and Percent

2) Click **Insert** in the menu bar

3) Click **Recommended Charts** in the Insert Ribbon

4) **Find the chart that represents the Pareto Chart.** It will most likely be the Clustered Column chart

5) Click **OK**

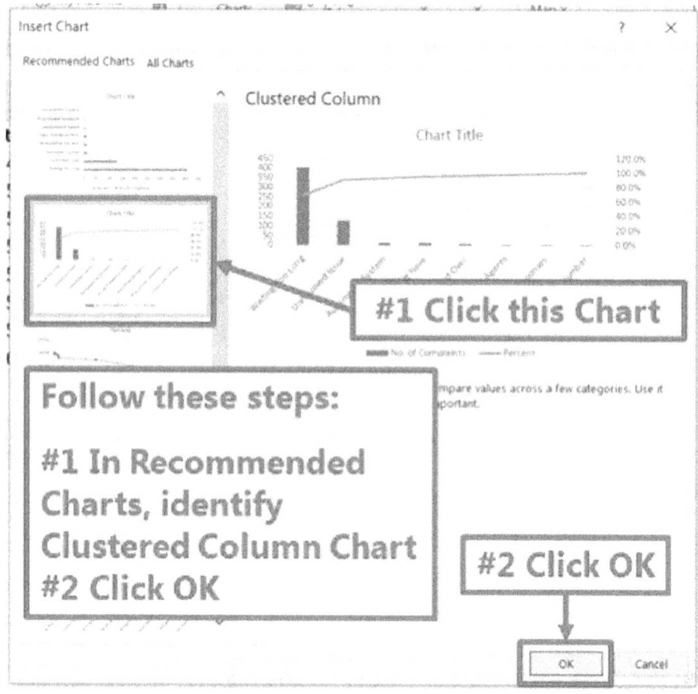

Step 3.3: Format your chart: Change the Gap Width between Bars

1) **Left click on any one of the bars**

2) Then **right click**

3) Click **Format Data Series**

Step 3.4: Format your chart: Change the Gap Width between Bars

1) Change the **Gap width to 10%**

Step 3.5: Format your chart: Label Cumulative Line

1) Click anywhere on the Cumulative Line

2) Click the **Plus (+) Sign** that appears on the top-right of the chart

3) Click **Data Labels**

Step 3.5: Format your chart: Label Cumulative Line

1) **Click on any data label** above the bar chart

2) In the **Format Data Labels** window, click **Above**

Step 3.6: Format your chart: Label the Bars

1) Click anywhere on the bars

2) Click the **plus (+) sign** on the top-right corner of the chart

3) Put the **check mark in Data Labels**

4) Data Labels for the bars will appear. We have cleaned the look of the data labels for cumulative line.

Your Pareto Chart is Complete.

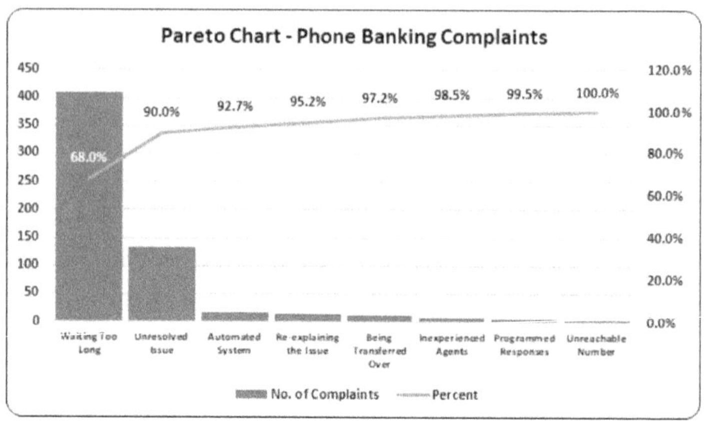

CHAPTER 7: REAL LIFE ANECDOTE # 3

Here I share another real-life story of how Pareto Analysis had a massive impact to solve a business problem.

The Story Begins

I was working as a Six Sigma professional with an India based Data Storage company. There were about 300 employees in this business process. When business customers faced a challenge, they would call the 800 number and these calls were managed by these employees. This was a fairly new process and due to the tight timelines of getting the process ready to handle customer calls, the standard operating procedures were not documented yet. An employee was hired, put through the process training, and was made to take these calls. This was the general protocol.

After about 3 months, the business owner found that this team has very high handle time of each call. Now, in a call centre, the Average Handle Time is considered an important metric. If the Average Handle Time is high, the below situations occur:

1) It results in longer time to resolve customer issue.
2) Callers wait in queue to speak to a telephone agent for

significantly longer time than expected and you know, it is a sin to keep your customers waiting to talk to someone.

3) More employees are needed to take calls.

4) If your competitor provides a better and faster service, your customers will switch to them making you lose business, lose market share, lose revenue, and lose reputation too.

So, our objective was to reduce the Average Handle Time to bring it down from 23 minutes to 15 minutes.

The Analysis

In the first three months of any human related business process, the data is generally not stable. This is because as humans learn new process, they keep getting better. Hence, you will see an upward movement in the data points. It is generally between 3 to 6 months that the data turns out to be stable. So, being dependent on the data to identify the root-causes was not a wise choice.

In this scenario, our team decided to survey the agents who were taking calls. The survey asked them the reasons of high handle time. Since they are hands on, it was expected that their inputs will be insightful. And so, they were.

Many inputs came in. People said the call taking time was high because of:

1) Difficult customers
2) Lack of Job knowledge
3) Communication Issues
4) System latency
5) Non-standardized protocols, among others

We did a Pareto Analysis and here was the result:

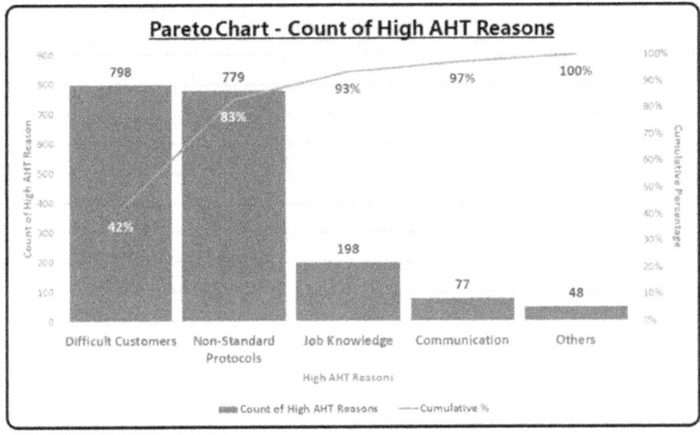

Interpreting the Chart and Identifying the Root-Cause

Difficult customers contributed to 42% of the responses and Non-Standard Protocols was the second highest with 41% responses. Both contributed to 83% of total responses.

Action Identification and Implementation

Now, when you want to improve a business process, you can create actions for only those root-causes which are in your direct control. You cannot work on those which are not in your direct control. Difficult customers were not in our direct control. But Non-Standard Protocols to handle the transactions or calls was something that we could work on.

As every organization has limited resources, we too faced that challenge. We were limited on manpower, subject matter experts, and the time we could take to resolve the issue.

So, we only had to find those transaction types that contributed the highest volume of calls. No price for guessing which tool did we use for this. It was Pareto Chart.

We decided to create standardized protocols for only those transaction types that are high in number. So, we pulled the data, created a pareto chart and identified that OAM Pass and OAM Fail were the top two types of calls that contributed to 73% of volume.

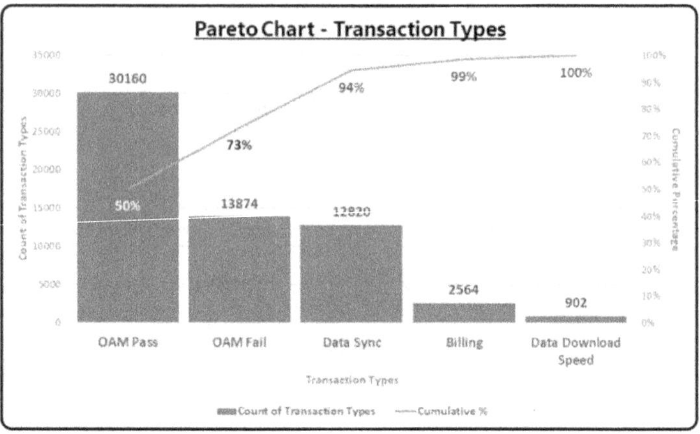

The training team and the subject matter experts went to the drawing board. They created step-by-step instruction document to resolve customer queries for these two transaction types. And they trained all the 300 employees to follow the step-by-step guide.

Results

In about 3 weeks, the Average Handle Time dropped well below the target. The business owner was delighted to see the targeted efforts taken by the team. The team (although new) was proud of their achievement. As usual, my boss loved the complimentary email drafted by the business owner. He was happy, my department was happy, and I was happy too. Now, I could ask for not just an increment but a promotion too. Lol.

A simple Pareto Analysis came to rescue once more. And this time we used it multiple times, first to identify the root-cause, and then to identify the top transaction type that had maximum volume.

And we come to the end of this real-life anecdote. I hope you liked it. Do share your feedback.

ABOUT THE AUTHOR

Rahul G. Iyer, the Founder, CEO and Lead Trainer of Advanced Innovation Group Pro Excellence (AIGPE), is a professional with over 19 years of total experience. Out of which, 16 years has been dedicated to the field of Quality, Process Improvements, and Project Management. He is a Certified Six Sigma Master Black Belt (MBB), a Certified Six Sigma Black Belt, Lean Specialist, Project Management Professional, Certified Scrum Master, Certified ISO 9001 Auditor, has completed his MBA in Operations and is Graduated with Mathematics Honors. Rahul has worked with several Fortune 500 organizations world-wide, executing 700+ Six Sigma, Lean, and Project Management projects, and saving billions of dollars for them. He has also trained and coached professionals for over 10,000 hours.

Rahul lives with his family in Pune, India. He is an absolute foody, loves superhero movies, and is a history buff.

His past full-time role was at the Bank of New York Mellon.

His worked as a Vice President and during his stint of over 11 years, he served as the Head of Data and Analytics for Real Estate Portfolio Management, Head of Transformation Academy, Head of the PMO Office for Transformation and Program Management, and he also managed and several Lean Six Sigma projects in the capacity of a Master Black Belt leading a team of Six Sigma Black Belts.

Rahul has won several awards including the International Team Excellence Award (executed by American Society for Quality) for the Best Project Category.